UNITED WE STAND

Leadership Stories for a New Decade

Written by
KEITH MARTINO

ISBN-13: 978-0-9791669-9-0

Copyright © January 20, 2020
by Keith Martino

All rights reserved. No part of this publication may be reproduced, distributed, or transmitted in any form or by any means, including photocopying, recording, or other electronic or mechanical methods, without the prior written permission of the publisher, except in the case of brief quotations embodied in critical reviews and certain other noncommercial uses permitted by copyright law.

For permission requests, write to the publisher, addressed

"Attention: Permissions Coordinator,"

at the address below.

CMI Assessments

P.O. Box 703803

Dallas, TX 75370-3803

www.CMIAssessments.com

Also by Keith Martino

Leadership Books
EXPECT Leadership – The Executive Edition
Short Stories for Busy Leaders

Leadership Guides
EXPECT Leadership in Business
EXPECT Leadership in Engineering
EXPECT Leadership in Technology

Sales Handbooks
Get Results
Results Now
Selling to Americans

This book is dedicated to my mother, Ruth Gwinn Martino. She lived every day

to glorify our Most Gracious and Loving Heavenly Father.

May we enthusiastically follow in her footsteps.

Keith Martino

January 20, 2020

O Lord, the God of my master Abraham,

if you are planning to make my mission a success,

please guide me in a special way.

Genesis 24:42 (NLT)

The Purpose of This Book

United We Stand:

This book demonstrates a variety of ways to build a stronger, more cohesive team that consistently achieves excellent results.

The Overarching Theme:

Our colleagues, friends and family instinctively examine our true character and motives more closely than we imagine. The more transparent we become, the greater our probability for unity, innovation and repeat success.

Each story reminds us that daily words and actions define and refine your legacy as a leader.

So why spotlight these points in advance?

We want you and your team to get the most out of every story.

As you reflect on each humorous or insightful instance, look for the ways each person reveals and telegraphs their character through their actions and reactions to others.

As we said at FedEx:

"Transparency inspires courage, responsibility and discretionary effort!"

United We Stand

Table of Contents

STORY 1: You Can't Hide Your Leadership Talent 11

STORY 2: Model Leadership in a Crisis 25

STORY 3: Can You Recover From a Temper Tantrum? 37

STORY 4: Time to Approach the Boss? 47

STORY 5: How to Lead When You're Under Fire 61

STORY 6: Are Your Employees Thirsty for Feedback? 75

STORY 7: How to Manage Difficult Employees 87

STORY 8: How to Pick Your Next Leader 101

Keep In Mind *(Concluding Comments)* 109

Dedication – A Tiny Leader Stands Tall 111

Closing – Sometimes It Takes a Bluegrass Village 115

Acknowledgements 123

STORY

. . . . .

1

You Can't Hide Your Leadership Talent

*Make humility
your team's heartbeat.*

Nicos never looks like a man of means.

Some days he dresses like a hobo.

Yet something about his gait caught my eye and commanded my attention. His humble stature and understated persona triggered my curiosity. And the quiet confidence he exuded made me dare to venture out across a dimly lit street one night in the Principality of Monaco. I needed help. Nicos was on a mission to remain discreet.

Now let's contrast Nicos with the royal family of Monaco just two blocks away. Princess Caroline and her crew built their

Casino de Monte-Carlo cascading down the hilltop.

Envious jetsetters drive a long stream of Maserati, Rolls-Royce, and Bentley convertibles down the Grand Prix past the casino every day hoping to be noticed by royalty. Many luscious yards are manicured with fountains and water features to make them stand out.

So why was I scrambling so hard to catch up with such a meek stranger in the midst of all of this opulence? I wasn't sure.

In some ways, this man appeared to be the least likely source for the highbrow insight we sought that evening. And yet, there I was. Seeking his counsel. And when I caught up, he didn't seem surprised.

"Excuse me, sir! My wife and I are searching for the perfect restaurant to celebrate a special occasion in Monte Carlo. Have you ever heard of this place?" Pointing toward a French name I could barely pronounce, he smiled quietly.

"Yes, I remember that one. It's a few blocks that way," he said as he motioned toward the distance. He strode off quickly with a wave and slight chuckle. I never thought we'd encounter him again.

As we arrived at the restaurant, there he was. Nicos, the man I'd just spoken to. I was stunned! He was standing outside the front door and about to enter. Since he was all alone, we invited him over to our table. Throughout the evening he entertained and enlightened us with stories about Cyprus, his native country. Some stories were funny. Some were uncomfortably sad.

The thing I remember most distinctly about his message that night was his strong yearning to bring the people of Cyprus and the citizens of the United States into a deeper and more trusting relationship. Nicos literally wept for the Cypriots whom he felt would never experience the quality of life he dreamed imaginable. He felt that building an alliance between the governments of the U.S. and his country was essential for their future. He seemed to have

Your Leadership Talent / 1

influence in Cyprus. Still, we had no idea who he was.

Several years later, I visited Cyprus because Nicos worked so hard to stay in touch with us. I gulped as he showed me his beachfront acreage along the southern coastline of Larnaca. I snapped pictures of his 10-story office building in the heart of the capitol city. Everywhere we went, people stopped Nicos and asked questions about financial planning. I felt smarter just standing beside him.

Nicos' modesty was consistent throughout the time I was in his country. His lack of self-importance was always disarming, but his factual presentation was persuasive. His humility was authentic. That I knew for sure.

And then ... The Greek Wedding
The night before I left Cyprus, Nicos invited me to join him at a wedding for his friend's daughter. Nicos apologized to me and said that he needed to be there and asked me to join him. Sure, I thought, still looking for any opportunity to learn more about my

mysterious acquaintance. I was due to leave the island soon and still didn't have a clear view of why he was so revered. After all, I'd met Nicos by chance in the shadows of Monaco.

The wedding was a lavishly appointed affair with a full band and a head table for the most honored guests. There were hundreds of attendees at this five-course wedding dinner.

As we were ushered in, the father of the bride insisted that Nicos sit beside him and his wife at the head table. Nicos politely declined again and again. He and I instead sat at an understated table off to the side of the room. Nothing he did seemed to change the bestowed level of adulation toward Nicos. Throughout the evening people kept coming over to him and asking him questions in Greek about their banks and their money.

You can imagine his chagrin when they stopped the band during dinner to propose a special Greek toast in Nicos' honor. Still I wasn't sure whom I was sitting beside. I only recognized that this group of Cypriots considered

Leaders Can Be Humble.

Nicos to be a most highly esteemed guest.

Departing Cyprus, I realized there were many things I still didn't know about Nicos. He downplayed his status. I didn't know how he came by his wealth. I wasn't sure how he got into the business of developing multi-purpose office complexes with attached hotels. I wasn't even sure I could properly spell his last name. Yet I knew that Nicos was a leader of the highest order.

The people of Cyprus had spoken. Their choice was Nicos. I had a long flight home to contemplate what I had learned.

Three Lessons From Nicos Demetriou:

1. **Leaders can be humble.** It doesn't detract from their inherent gift of leadership. Even when Nicos put on his most low-profile attire to downplay his influence, the people who knew him best sought him out most often. They trusted his ability to help shape their decisions. He was a leader among leaders. His gift was obvious.

Leaders Who Use Their Gifts To Help Unite Other People Are Loved.

People Respect Leaders Who Value Others Ahead of Themselves.

2. Leaders who use their gifts to help unite other people are loved. Those who choose to divide and conquer pay a fatal price for their divisive leadership style. As do their teams, their companies and their families. In every endeavor, "United we stand. Divided we fall."

3. People respect leaders who value others ahead of themselves. The old cliché, "People don't care how much you know until they know how much you care," applied to Nicos. He was a leader because he put the interest of his colleagues ahead of himself. I remember how he wept at the thought of his fellow citizens living in less than optimal conditions.

As you read through this book, we hope you will be moved by the spirit of unity that leaders like Nicos inspire.

Nicos never looks like a man of means. Some days he dresses like a hobo.

Yet Nicos can never conceal the gift of leadership that he possesses.

Neither can YOU!

STORY

. . . . .

2

Model Leadership in a Crisis

Two sides to the story?
Find common goals.

Imagine my skyrocketing pulse when I got the news: "Jim Barksdale is on the line for you. He sounds angry!"

My heart sank. Jim Barksdale was chief operating officer at FedEx. Many of my comrades on our FedEx management team respected Jim almost as much as they loved our founder, Fred Smith. I was one of Jim's biggest fans.

I hastily grabbed the phone, and he launched into a passionate tirade. "Do we have a guy on our global sales team named Rick?"

"Yes," I stammered.

"Well, you need to FIRE him!" he exclaimed.

Not a great salutation. I assumed Jim wasn't having his best day. The rap got worse. Jim had just returned from lunch with an important FedEx customer. The customer had skewered Jim for an hour regarding Rick's demeanor. They made him seem like a price-gouging villain. They complained about Rick's lack of attentiveness, described him as arrogant, and then topped off the discussion by saying they would likely switch over to our largest competitor. I quickly agreed to check into the matter. Still shaking, I thanked him for calling.

Little did Jim know that Rick was in my Texas town for a strategic planning session. He was waiting unsuspectingly down the hall. All eyes were upon me as I walked back into the meeting.

"What did he want?" someone asked, as I entered the room.

"He said I should fire Rick immediately." I responded.

Everyone looked at Rick. Rick froze in mid-sentence. You could see the blood slowly drain out of Rick's face as the gravity of Jim's phone call set in. He seemed to want to say something, but his lips didn't move. Stunned speechless was an understatement. Rick was mortified.

"Rick, you and I have only one choice if you want to save your job. We need to be on the first flight to Memphis in the morning." Rick agreed.

We were perched in Jim Barksdale's office when he arrived the next day. He looked at the two of us and invited us to come in to talk.

I had seen Jim in many pleasant situations, but this wasn't one of those. It wasn't an awards ceremony or a celebration dinner. It was to be the scene of a very important sequence of leadership lessons that I would never forget.

The following three lessons will serve you well in a crisis:

Get the Facts.

Make a Positive Difference.

Lesson one: STOP! Discern the facts before taking action.

Jim methodically stepped Rick through the details of his customer encounter and then turned the floor over to us. I spoke up and made a case for Rick's reputation. It wasn't eloquent, but it was sincere. Jim listened intently and then asked for Rick's side of the story. When Rick finished, Jim wasn't angry anymore. In fact, he was feeling pretty good about the manner in which Rick had handled the customer's unreasonable expectations. Jim *listened*.

Lesson two: Once you have clarity, take action and make a positive difference.

Jim weighed all of the details and spun around in his chair to make another phone call. *Who is he calling now?*, I wondered silently. The senior executive that Jim had dined with the day before answered the phone. Jim apologized for the early morning call and proceeded to set an appointment for Rick to meet with the customer the following day. He used his influence to get Rick back into the dialogue without making the customer angry.

Model the Leadership You Expect.

It was a riveting display of professionalism and persuasive positioning.

Lesson three: Model the leadership you expect from others.

Jim apologized to Rick for having assumed that the story the customer shared with him was gospel. He explained that he had violated his own policy of always pursuing both sides of every incriminating story. He thanked Rick for stepping up to the plate and visiting him immediately when the pressure was on.

In short: Jim listened with an open mind. He took action to correct his mistake. He demonstrated humility and moved us forward. More important, he modeled the leadership style he expected from us. Rick met with the customer and ultimately turned the situation into a game plan that deepened the relationship between FedEx and their company.

Jim Barksdale later became CEO of Netscape until it merged with AOL – and then he became quite wealthy. Never one to miss an opportunity to help, Jim took a portion of his estate and established a foundation to equip underprivileged kids with literacy skills. I went back to Dallas and thought about my unexpected trip to Memphis and what Jim had

Lead with Humility and Model Professionalism in your Words and Actions.

taught me in that brief span of time.

Think about it. When the world seems to be imploding and you don't understand why employees seem to be conducting themselves in a counterproductive way, get the facts.

Listen with an open mind to both sides of the story. Take action in a positive manner by leveraging your most persuasive abilities to move the situation forward.

Lead with humility and model professionalism in your words and actions.

Imagine my skyrocketing pulse when I got the news: "Jim Barksdale is on the line for you."

I would love to get that call again today.

. . . . .

"Model Leadership in a Crisis" was featured in *AZ **Big Media*** magazine.

STORY

. . . . .

3

Can You Recover From a Temper Tantrum?

*If you make a mistake,
fix it.*

Joan storms out of the office. The door slams. And everything comes to a screeching halt.

The meeting has barely begun. Now, it's over. Today there will be minimal progress generated by this senior-level sales team. Why? The leader has blown her lid and lost the respect of her managers in one flaming fait accompli. What a way to start the week!

Nancy, who is most distraught about the situation, speaks up in a lame attempt to ease the tension. No use. Team momentum is shot.

Who Among Us Hasn't Lost Our Smile Over Someone Else's Dumb Mistake?

Slowly but surely, the seasoned leaders wander out of this conference room dazed and confused over what might come from this latest tirade. The bottom line: That momentary flash point rapidly digresses into a wasted day for eight highly paid executives. Calculate the math: One minute of unbridled fury unleashed by the top leader on eight executives can cost the company at least 64 hours of plummeting productivity in just one full workday. Important decisions are delayed. Timid personalities are traumatized. Who knows the true cost of such an ego-fueled stunt! The lingering effect is deadly.

Yet, who among us hasn't lost our smile over someone else's dumb mistake?

We've all made our share of blunders and let our anger get the best of us. But when leaders blow their cool over a minor incident, it's a BIG deal. Every time!

EXPONENTIAL MULTIPLYING FACTOR

Why? Just call it the exponential multiplying factor (EMF). And whether you like it or not, EMF is alive and well in your company.

The Negative Exertion of Power Triggers an Exaggerated Reaction.

Suddenly Your Team Will Begin Hesitating on Making Timely Decisions.

As a senior executive, remember that sudden negative exertion of power triggers an exaggerated reaction further down the food chain. Remember the man who kicks the dog? The dog then turns and bites the cat. And so it goes.

You can trigger EMF in a millisecond. Recovering from such an instantaneous combustion takes a lot more time. Depending on the topic, it may require months or years for us to reestablish our positive presence in the minds of employees. And, they'll never let on that we are still in catch-up mode. It will just be understood by the masses. They have long memories.

They'll smile. They'll laugh at your jokes. They'll say flattering things to your face. And just below the surface they'll be waiting for your next shoe to drop. You'll recognize the signs of the aftershock. Suddenly, your team will begin hesitating on making timely decisions. They will avoid difficult conversations that need to take place, and will allow your competition to walk away with your business because no one wants to tell you (the boss) any bad news.

You Can Turn Your Isolated Slip Into a Teachable Moment.

Practice the Art of Recovery.

RECOVERY MODE

So, how can you recover from an embarrassing faux pas? Here are three suggestions:

1) Try your best to avoid expressing your anger in a group when your frustration is really disappointment with one specific person.

2) If you make such a mistake in front of a group, quickly and sincerely apologize to your team. Just as importantly, ask the individual who has sparked your ire to talk with you in private after the meeting. Let everyone within earshot hear your subtle request.

3) Make a point to rapidly change the topic of the conversation to something positive. Come back to the sensitive topic later in the discussion when you have regained your sense of humor.

Yes, you can turn your isolated slip into a teachable moment if you practice the art of recovery. But it requires some discipline on the leader's part. First, you must limit these occurrences to rare incidents with diminishing frequency. Secondly, you must honestly admit mistakes when you make them. This enables

- **Limit the Occurrences.**

- **Admit Your Mistakes.**

- **Set a New Tone.**

direct reports and others to see that you understand your own human frailties and that you, too, are seeking to grow in your leadership responsibilities. Your reaction to your own angry outbursts sets the tone for your team. Turn a negative moment into a lasting memory! Imagine this.

Joan storms out of the office. The door slams. And everything comes to a screeching halt.

Then realizing the impact on her subordinates, Joan turns on her heels. She steps back into the room with an embarrassed smile. She apologizes to the group for her hasty and misguided behavior. She invites the person who sparked her anger to discuss the matter in private. And she reengages the group in a positive direction that results in congratulating someone in the group for a job well done.

Now that's the shot you want "heard 'round the world"!

. . . . .

"Can You Recover From a Temper Tantrum?" was featured in **Modern Contractor Solutions** magazine.

STORY

4

Time to Approach the Boss?

*The future is bright
when you move past the past.*

Jenn boards Southwest Flight 690 from Dallas Love Field to La Guardia.

There aren't many passengers aboard the plane this morning. She understands why. It seems painfully early.

As Jenn strolls down the aisle, she is delighted to find her favorite exit seat available. After experiencing unexpected drama in airport security, she wants to slip away into quiet anonymity far from TSA scrutiny. But, just as Jenn settles into her comfy little spot, the flight attendant presses the intercom button and

Each Plane is Evenly Balanced For Optimum Safety and Efficiency.

asks several passengers to do something unconscionable.

The attendant asks them to move.

Move??? No thanks! Not this Jenn.

Jenn feels her day spiraling south and it isn't even 6:00 a.m.

She's tempted to slip her headphones on and feign deep sleep. She considers denying that she understands English, her native tongue. She even ponders whether they might believe her seatbelt latch is inexplicably stuck.

She feels certain of one thing: she isn't about to move. It isn't fair!

But then she hears a soft voice from a familiar past. And she remembers every airline's weight and balance precautions from her former FedEx career. The folks at FedEx are meticulous about loading every aircraft properly. Tremendous importance is placed on having each plane evenly balanced for optimum safety and efficiency. And while this 737 seems massive, a disproportionate cluster of passengers in the middle of the plane still

A lot of Managers & Employees Are in the "Wrong Seat" On the "Right Plane".

matters. An improper balance will compromise the plane's performance.

You see, Jenn is on the right plane, but in the wrong seat from the captain's perspective.

What does this have to do with the balance of talent on your team?

Over the years, Jenn has seen a lot of managers and employees in the "wrong seat" on the right plane.

They loved their company. They were loyal. They were committed. But they weren't suited to perform best in the role they were currently assigned. And in most cases, they weren't having fun.

It happens often. And it often happens for good reason.

Take Jenn's friend, Steve, for instance.

Steve is an extraordinarily talented applications developer. Clients love him. Competitors fear him. And he was always being recognized for solving tough challenges for customers. In fact, Steve is so good, the president of his

That's When Performance Drops.

company promoted him to run the IT department.

That's when Steve's life fell apart.

And then there was Jenn's buddy, Brian, from Chicago.

Brian is a good plant manager. But it was mostly because he inherited a solid team. Brian's CEO assumed that since Brian is a competent plant manager, he'd make a great chief operating officer.

That was when Brian's world caved in.

And Jenn remembers her neighbor, JT. JT was, at one time, a pretty good lawyer. Then he decided to go run his family company's largest branch office in order to gain operating experience.

It wasn't a pretty picture.

Profitability plummeted. Employees quit. And the very best managers under JT began dusting off their resumes.

Jenn could list others with similar "seating" dilemmas, but I'm sure you get the point.

How Do You Know If You're in the Right Seat On Your Company's Plane?

Different Seat / 4

Which brings us to the question:

Is it time to talk with the boss about finding a more valuable way to contribute to your team?

You may not be certain you're in the right seat on your company plane. If that's the case, take a proactive approach. You'll be glad you did.

Here are five angles to consider.

(Yes = 2 Pts / No = 0 Pts / Not Sure = 1 Pt)

Respond honestly to gauge if you are in the right role to achieve maximum success.

1) I'm having fun in my current position. ____ **pts**

2) I experience consistent, measurable success. ____ **pts**

3) My boss expresses appreciation for my work. ____ **pts**

4) Teammates express appreciation of my role. ____ **pts**

5) Relationships with co-workers improve daily. ____ **pts**

**When You're in the Right Seat,
You Feel the Momentum
of Your Contribution.**

Results

7+ Pts = Congratulations! You will likely be successful in this position.

5-6 Pts = Talk with management about what you can do to prepare for a different role. Explain that you want to contribute in the most beneficial way. Perhaps reconsider a prior role where you excelled.

1-4 Pts = Your days may be numbered unless something changes. Look for another position in your existing company ASAP!

Now let's look at your potential move from 30,000 feet.

When you're in the right seat on the plane, the results and enjoyment are obvious to everyone. You feel the momentum of your contribution and you're often surprised by how receptive teammates and management appear to be.

It's Worth the Effort to Find a Different Role Where You Can Succeed.

When you are in the wrong seat, life and work become a drag on your enjoyment. It may take time in your company to find a different role where you can succeed, but it's worth the effort.

The morning that Jenn boarded Flight 690 to New York, she wasn't considering how she might be impacting the safety and flight balance of the Southwest aircraft.

Once she made the timely decision to move to another seat, everyone seemed at ease. And she had a fantastic flight! The number one rule in aviation is, "Fly safely, every flight!"

Perhaps now is the best time for you to change seats.

Fly safely, every flight!

. . . .

"Time to Approach the Boss" was featured in ***Women in Technology International.***

STORY

. . . . .

5

How to Lead When You're Under Fire

Take the hit.
Come back strong.

His casual comment made me gulp.

"What do you MEAN they flipped this bad boy upside down?" I whispered to the pilot.

We were seated aboard a fully loaded FedEx DC-10.

Up to this point, I had been carefully strapping myself into the tight quarters of a cockpit jump seat directly behind his. Suddenly I was wishing I had just flown commercial.

As the captain nonchalantly reminded the copilot of that fateful April afternoon, I thought about the long haul we were about to launch from Memphis to London.

"Yep, this is the first time they've officially put this puppy back into service since *that flight*. I think it should be okay," the first officer stammered with some hesitation.

Though it was nearly 2 a.m., I was now wide awake.

I remembered the incident. Thousands of our FedEx employees around the globe celebrated the heroic team from that historic Flight 705. The crew had miraculously wrestled the plane away from the would-be hijacker and lived to tell about it. Now I was getting an inside view of the refurbished fuselage on the FedEx jet we had often discussed.

But the gift kept giving.

"This is it. We're about to test this airplane's viability under normal use," restated the captain.

News to me! *In the middle of the night? Over the ocean?* I mumbled to myself. I was still trying hard to look collected like a seasoned member of the crew, but I was struggling.

Lead Under Fire / 5

Deep down, I didn't recall signing up for this test spin.

My thoughts flashed back to the headlines and trial of the disgruntled employee who boarded this same FedEx cargo plane bound for San Jose and attacked the crew, his fellow employees. Armed with a speargun and a couple of small sledgehammers, he had commandeered the plane. In his mind, he was headed back to the company's corporate Super Hub to slam into a silo farm storing hundreds of thousands of gallons of jet fuel.

His goal? To wipe out his employer and get revenge.

Ultimately, we learned that those former FedEx aviators were so disabled by the tragedy that they were never able to pilot again. Yet they remain heroes because they instinctively reacted as a cohesive and unified team under the stress of an unanticipated attack.

They saved the plane. They saved the cargo. They saved the company. And they saved the city from a cataclysmic catastrophe.

Winners Instinctively React to Challenges as a Cohesive Team.

How many lives were spared? We'll never know.

But, their air battle is legendary. You'll find the heart-stopping details in the book *Hijacked: The True Story of the Heroes of Flight 705* by David Hirschman. Here's a sampling as told masterfully by the author:

> David Sanders, Jim Tucker, and Andy Peterson had taken off on a regular "out-and-back," delivering and picking up packages for FedEx's next-day service. They had one jumpseat passenger, an off-duty colleague who they assumed was simply taking advantage of the FedEx perk allowing virtually all employees to ride the company jets for free. ...

With superhuman strength and fueled by sheer fury, the attacker struck the pilots again and again.

What he didn't count on was the skill and intelligence of the pilots. While Sanders and Peterson tried to stop the relentless battering, copilot Tucker swung the

Friendly Fire is Unfortunately Too Common.

It Didn't Occur to Me That

I was Actually In the

Hijacker's Seat.

aircraft into dangerous flight maneuvers in an attempt to literally knock the man off his feet. ... Such maneuvers take enormous mastery and concentration even under the best of circumstances.*

As I sat there in the cockpit months later, I was fixated on the wings that were nearly sheared off the sides of the plane in which I was sitting. It didn't occur to me that I was actually in the hijacker's seat.

So what do you do when you're knocked down by someone from your own team?

Friendly fire is unfortunately too common. Intentional or unintentional. In battle and in life. It has been estimated that there may have been as many as 8,000 friendly fire incidents in the Vietnam War alone. Friendly fire is defined as an inadvertent attack by a military force on friendly or neutral troops, while attempting to attack the enemy. It can also occur in families.

In the corporate world, you've observed friendly fire leveled between teammates. It has stopped many great teams, companies, and

How Do You Respond When You Find Yourself Under Siege?

critical endeavors short of their goal. This book is being written to head off the frustration and emotional buildup that can sometimes lead to friendly fire.

But the real question is personal: How do you respond when you find yourself under siege by a fellow leader? Do you lunge back? Do you outgun your colleague? Do you throw your hands up and quit?

Take it from the pilots of Flight 705. Regardless of what is said or done by a peer:

Keep your cool. Unite the group. Focus everyone on the mission.

Your positive leadership will accomplish what only the most courageous leaders dare strive to achieve. Your team will deliver a solution to the challenges that are threatening the project and will restore unity across the team. That's successful leadership.

When the situation is resolved, your leadership will have made the difference. You'll know you overcame your own temptation to

Keep Your Cool.

Unite the Group.

Focus Everyone on the Mission.

fire back. Your team and your mission are too valuable to sacrifice on the altar of ego.

Yes, that was quite a memorable flight for many reasons.

His casual comment made me gulp.

"What do you MEAN they flipped this bad boy upside down?" I whispered to the pilot.

As I sat perched behind the captain, he reflected on the bottom line one more time.

"They fought to save more than their lives. They did it for you and me."

I got it.

Keep your cool. Unite the group. Focus everyone on the mission.

. . . .

Inside cover comments from Hijacked: The True Story of the Heroes of Flight 705 *by Dave Hirschman. Available on Amazon.com.*

STORY

·····

6

Are Your Employees Thirsty for Feedback?

*Small things
are still the big things.*

Juan is a quiet, reflective guy. He's also a musician's musician.

And when it's sizzling hot during the summer months, Juan's instincts are right on target. He knows instinctively that certain employee needs must always be quenched. Yes, his roofing crew needs water, but just as desperately Juan knows his direct reports need to know he cares. Perhaps it seems odd to link these seemingly disparate issues so closely. I'll explain.

The first time I saw Juan leading a corporate

As We Become More Technical, Many Leaders Have Forgotten That Every Employee Needs the Human Touch.

business discussion it was mid-July. Juan was emphasizing the criticality of consistent hydration to a team of beleaguered roofers. That's right. He was discussing the natural healing properties of water. Not the benefits of Big Red, Rockstar or Monster Energy. Water!

I watched the compassion with which he conveyed his message. I sensed the appreciation that washed across the faces of his employees. They were drenched and relieved that he appreciated the reality of their hot workplace. After all, they were only human. Aren't we all?

The metal roof manufacturing plant in which Juan plays a pivotal role leans heavily on sophisticated physics, control system integration and efficient processes. The paint line Juan oversees each day depends on management's knowledge of polymers, chemistry equations and the aerodynamics of heat dissipation. But most of all, it relies upon leaders who care.

So, what's the message?

As we become more and more technically oriented, many company leaders have forgotten that every employee needs the human touch –

The Thirst for Targeted Instantaneous Feedback is Growing.

Team Members are Fiercely Loyal When They are Treated Like Individuals with Unique Goals & Objectives.

a routine dose from a boss who cares. And the thirst for targeted instantaneous feedback is growing exponentially. On a rooftop or in an office.

The great news is that the Internet Generation constantly reminds us of emotional needs with frequent requests for validation and confirmation. While they may be technically proficient beyond their years, they yearn as desperately as any other generation for someone to say "good job!"

And while we sometimes laugh about participation trophies for everyone on the team, the truth is that they are fiercely loyal when treated like individuals with unique goals and objectives. A healthy corporate culture is particularly important to this next generation. Treat them right and you will be amazed by their contribution.

Here are five questions you can ask yourself about your corporate culture to know if the human element is being given enough attention in your company:

Is the Human Element Being Given Enough Attention In Your Company?

1. When we walk through a job site or office corridor, do we generally see smiles on the faces of colleagues?
2. Do we take time to celebrate the successes of our team and our team members?
3. Do we typically thank each other for the help we receive from one another?
4. Do we promptly apologize when we realize we failed to live up to a commitment?
5. Do we usually take time to encourage one another when the challenges are fierce?

If you answered yes to **four** of the five questions, you should go back and encourage your team to keep it up! You have a very special workplace where the stage is set for success. Thank each person for the active role they play in making your workplace friendly.

If you answered yes to **three** of the five questions, you are on the way to building a rock-solid team. Now press a little further and ask for suggestions from your boss, peers and direct reports on how to take your group to the next level of camaraderie. It may be as simple as encouraging everyone to practice public

If You Answered Yes to *Only One* of the Five Questions, You Will Have a Hard Time Retaining Young Talent.

recognition of a peer who has achieved a recent accomplishment. That's a fun exercise to build momentum!

If you answered yes to **two** of the five questions, you may want to talk with senior management about ideas to build collaboration, teamwork and stronger loyalty to your company. You can be a leader for the cause by introducing positive articles and ideas on a regular basis despite any push back you may encounter. Your company will need a makeover in order to hang on to good talent in the future.

If you answered yes to **only one** of the five questions, you will have a hard time retaining young talent. Before you throw in the towel, it may be time for a little self-examination. Is there a possibility that you too have fallen into the rut of ignoring the foundational needs of your employees?

Perhaps it's time to plant your feet firmly in place and commit to helping reshape the environment in which you and your team can thrive. After all, they say the best time to plant a tree was twenty years ago. The second-best time is today. Act now!

Balance Technology & Humanity. Show You Care!

Thirsty for Feedback / 6

I spoke to Juan last week. They have made vast improvements in the infrastructure of their company over the past year. Their profitability is at an all-time high and revenue growth is extraordinarily strong. The future looks brighter than ever for this fifty-year-old company.

Juan is a keyboard man.

And when the lights come up and the syncopated salsa rhythms rumble through the crowd, Juan comes alive. His energy, leadership skills, and musicality blend seamlessly to create a music that refreshes the soul. Sure, Juan likes a steady drumbeat. He loves a jazzy melody. But most of all, Juan lives to help his fellow man!

Juan balances technology and humanity in a company that cares. And if you answered "yes" to **five** out of five questions, send us an email and we may feature your company in an upcoming article like this. You are building a great leadership team!

·····

"Are Your Employees Thirsty for Feedback?" was featured in the ***Roofing Contractor's Association of Washington Newsletter.***

STORY

·····

7

How to Manage Difficult Employees

*Beware of
the predictable surprise.*

His team calls him "Dangerous Dave" for good reason.

Dave self implodes in a New York minute.

Perhaps it's that inappropriate comment Dave is prone to blurt out. Or maybe it's that significant lapse in his judgment that triggers the first domino. It doesn't matter. The explosion is immediate and the outcome is far-reaching. And as Dave's manager or teammate, you needn't wonder. You will be blindsided by the flying debris.

Oh, he's not a terrible person. In fact, Dave typically has the best of intentions. He's just

Beware of Dangerous Dave.

**When the Stakes are High,
The Carnage is Legendary.**

an eternal optimist. And he never seems to notice the aftershock following behind him. Dave has what you might call "intermittent blind spots." And he lives in a constant state of denial. My, that's a deadly combination!

To make matters worse, Dave's boss can seldom anticipate the timing of Dave's next calamitous move. Even more troubling, Dave won't bring a brewing catastrophe to anyone's attention. But in this age of the virtual water cooler, people still talk. And the delay between when Dave pulls the proverbial pin from a nearby hand grenade and the time his boss hears the explosion only adds to the collateral damage.

So why does Dave's team tolerate him?

It's simple. On nine days out of ten his contribution to his team is substantial. And every time he does something helpful, teammates are once again tempted to forget about his recent faux pas. But when Dave bungles it, he offsets every positive action he's taken in one fatal blow! And it's a vicious cycle.

The first time I met Dave he showed up at

How Do You Spot a Dangerous Dave?

our house out of nowhere. He instinctively made himself as comfortable as a long lost friend. It was a quiet summer evening. Dave spied our spinet piano in the corner parlor. Impulsively responding to some mysterious melody in his mind, Dave lunged and launched into a loud, busy boogie that rattled our rafters.

He never asked if we cared. He never considered our toddlers asleep in a room nearby. Dave was on a roll entertaining us! In his mind's eye he was Billy Joel the Piano Man! In our remembrance, he set off pandemonium.

I painfully learned over the next few years that Dave was and is semi-oblivious to the world in which he lives. He careens off the walls of life like a drunken bull in your mother's precious china cabinet.

Sure, Dave's technically awesome. But on a practical level, Dave is blind to the subtleties of his behavior. He doesn't mean any harm. He's just being Dave.

So, is there a Dangerous Dave darting down your hall?

Avoid Any Temptation to Promote a Dangerous Dave.

He Will Be More Lethal with More Responsibility.

Don't answer too quickly. The ramifications are worth considering.

When it comes to business, Dave is amazingly self-assured. He's a problem solver. In those magical moments when Dave saves the day, you want to hug him. But when the stakes are most high and you can least afford a miscue; the carnage Dave creates is legendary.

How can you spot a Dangerous Dave before he wreaks havoc in your living room or lobby?

Answer these ten questions and you'll know if you have one.

Think of the person you know who most resembles Dave. Ask yourself:

1. Do his jokes often strike a jangled nerve in an unsuspecting bystander?
2. Do you see evidence that his family's patience has worn thin?
3. In the past, have you considered promoting him but decided against it each time?
4. Do you feel sorry for the fact that he frequently undermines his own success?

5. Do you continue to discover new and different things that he can do?

6. Are you often tempted to give him just one more try?

7. Do your team members frequently surprise you with startling new stories about Dave?

8. Are you allowing your soft heart to guide your logic?

9. Has he randomly cost you a small fortune in unintended consequences?

10. Would you say "NO!" if he asked to marry your daughter?

If you answered yes to seven or more of these questions, here's the inconvenient truth. You can't afford to have Dave on your payroll. No matter how much you would love to rehabilitate him. It's not worth it.

Here's an even more sobering thought. You will likely have to fire Dave if you don't take action. So what can you do now if you are dead set on keeping your Dangerous Dave?

Here are five suggestions listed in order of importance:

1. Reassign any people who report directly to Dave so that you limit his legal liability.

2. Put Dave in charge of special projects with limited downside.

3. Role play any important customer interactions before Dave leaves the office.

4. Check behind Dave to ensure he's following agreed upon processes.

5. Avoid any temptation to promote Dave. He will be even more lethal with more responsibility.

Remember... A little power goes a long way in the mind of a Dangerous Dave!

I ran into Dave's ex-wife not long ago. She and I laughed about all of the good times we had enjoyed with Dave. There were many.

But there was a deep sadness in her spirit as she relayed her decision to finally divorce Dave. He, of course was off on a new adventure leaving his former family far behind.

**Don't Let Dave Shake
Your Confidence in You.**

I'd like to say Dave will learn how to handle life one day. And I'd like to say I'll soon leap tall buildings in a single bound.

But I'm reminded of the time a good friend approached Dave and begged him not to apply for another promotion. "Dave, you've tried managing people on two other occasions and it didn't work out. What did you learn from those experiences that will help you be more successful this time around?"

Dave turned. He stared upwards in thought. Then he asked, "What do you mean???"

His team calls him "Dangerous Dave" for good reason.

Dave self-implodes in a New York minute.

Don't let Dave shake your confidence in you!

.....

"How to Identify & Manage Difficult Employees" was featured in **Young Upstarts Magazine.**

STORY

·····

8

How to Pick Your Next Leader

*So goes the leader,
so goes the pack.*

Ron is one of the most polite individuals you'll ever encounter. You'll never feel intimidated by Ron's presence. He answers your questions as smoothly and predictably as the captain of a cruise ship. Within minutes of meeting Ron, you'll know why he was recently promoted within a large French holding company.

Ron is pragmatically aggressive. He picks his battles carefully and is only aggressive in business endeavors when he sees a clear course to the winner's cup. Then, and only then, does he press full throttle ahead. Ron prides himself in preparation, so just in case, there's always an adequate stash of life vests onboard.

Should Your Next Leader Be Someone Who Proceeds Circumspectively Like Ron?

Or Are You Looking for a Hunter, Like Rob?

But wait – before you rush out and hire Ron to be the captain of your ship, don't forget to consider Rob. He may be just what you need.

Rob's persona is larger-than-life. He works fast and loves trading sports cars. In a crowd of construction CEOs, he can come across as a big, lovable teddy bear. However, when a casual conversation with Rob turns toward business strategy, Rob will magically morph into a hungry grizzly. He'll show you how to eat your competition for lunch.

Should your next leader be someone who proceeds circumspectively like Ron? Or are you looking for someone who is a natural born hunter like Rob? Hint: If you need Rob but hire Ron, you'll likely be seriously disappointed. Your patience will be exhausted. On the other hand, hire Rob and you'd better hold on to your hat.

Rob will enthusiastically and methodically pass every other car on the track. He'll interject an energy you didn't know was possible into every employee who is able to hang on for the ride. At the end of the day, Rob will have created new business opportunities you never thought possible.

Although Their Names Sound Similar, Their Styles are Vastly Different.

Sure, Rob will occasionally break something, but when he puts your stock car back together it will run so much faster than before that you will be among the first to forgive him. Rob takes aggressive chances and then makes smart decisions based on the way the market appears to evolve. His ability to plan and execute simultaneously is uncanny. He shifts gears without flinching and leans into the turns. Ron, on the other hand, intuitively reaches for the caution flag.

Although their names sound similar, their styles are vastly different on a practical level. They each get the desired results when matched with the appropriate assignment. That's why absolute clarity about which style of leader your business will need is so crucial.

Here are a few questions to ponder that may help you consider various leadership styles:

- What are you trying to accomplish with your company?
- How important is creativity/innovation in your business?

Which is More Important to You: Growth, Stability or Something Else?

- Which is more important to you: growth, stability or something else?

- Do your key processes need incremental improvement or a complete overhaul?

- How much risk are you willing to accept to achieve your top objectives?

Another thing to consider when changing/hiring leaders is knowing your corporate culture. You want your corporate values to be firmly entrenched when you pass the torch.

Bottom Line:

Consider not only the qualities of the candidates you're interviewing and/or screening, but also look at the needs of your business. Survey the current climate and anticipate changes that might impact you in the future.

In short, don't hire Ron if who you really need and want is Rob.

.....

"How to Pick Your Next Leader" was featured in ***Floor Covering News.***

Concluding Comments

Keep In Mind

United We Stand:

This book demonstrates a variety of ways to build a stronger, more cohesive team that consistently achieves excellent results.

The Overarching Theme:

Our colleagues, friends and family instinctively examine our true character and motives more closely than we imagine. The more transparent we become, the greater our probability for unity, innovation and repeat success.

Each story reminds us that daily words and actions define and refine your legacy as a leader.

So why spotlight these points?

We want you and your team to get the most out of every story.

Now reflect on each humorous or insightful instance. Look for the ways each person reveals and telegraphs their character through their actions and reactions to others.

And Remember...

"Transparency inspires courage, responsibility and discretionary effort!"

A Tiny Leader Stands Tall

A Dedication to Ruth Gwinn Martino

August 7, 1931 – October 2, 2008

Ruth steers her baby blue sedan toward the deserted intersection. Heading home from a taxing day in the Federal Building, she looks right. She glances left. And then...

Wham!

Before she can blink or think, a truck swerves past her and dumps three gigantic cotton bales onto the hood of her new Buick. Her slight, 5-foot-2-inch frame ricochets off the steering wheel like a pinball. Her sunglasses fling onto the dash. And her new ride is crushed beyond recognition. That has to hurt!

Dazed but not confused, Ruth realizes her afternoon challenges aren't over. They have just begun. And Ruth is driven by a passion more powerful than an 8-cylinder engine.

The driver speeds off – oblivious to the destruction. Ruth steps out of her car into the August swelter. The irony of this blindsiding event is unmistakable. It couldn't have happened to a nicer and more resilient person. And it couldn't have happened to a more determined cotton enthusiast. Ruth will overcome many jarring jolts in life. This was just one such unexpected speed bump.

Dynamite Comes in Small Packages

Ruth humbly rose above the crowd as one of the first women to make a meaningful impact on her statewide agricultural scene. She secured funding for entrepreneurs who were willing to bet the farm on hard work and a hope for decent weather. She helped stabilize the environment by encouraging conservation when land use might have otherwise veered out of control.

She consistently modeled a willingness to go above and beyond to help the people she cherished. Sometimes it came at her expense. After all, how many people do you know who have been hit by a flying bale of cotton?

Though small in stature, large landowners affectionately called her Mrs. Ruth.

Every time she was nominated for a promotion, farmers, business leaders, and local bankers fought tooth and nail to support her. The respect was mutual and she was the first woman in her state agency to be named Executive Director.

Ironically, though her favorite car was crushed by a flurry of runaway cotton bales, Ruth still loved those who raised it by the acre. She never forgot the fleece-white fields from which she had come. Her siblings became large-scale agriculturalists before the trend became a global norm. Her youngest brother ran a regional cotton gin that grew quickly and employed family members and neighbors alike. An older brother died at a young age in an untimely granary accident.

Dedication

Years later, Ruth laughed about the devastation to her baby blue auto through clear azure eyes. Ruth's eyes were clear because her conscience was clean.

As I grew older and reflected on Ruth's unique family, I realized that they – the Gwinn family – were guided by an unspoken balance of principles that held true, regardless of their circumstances or hazards. They were among the most principled individuals I've met.

These principles were born out of the Great Depression. They survived World War II. And they offer clarity for those of us who seem destined to live in future decades of virtual reality, artificial intelligence, and rapid change.

I believe these simple values also provide refuge and direction for those of us who want to survive the turbulence of life to make a difference in our communities, our companies, and our families. I call these principles "The Gwinn Ten." I believe Ruth, my mother, would agree.

Thou Shalt Not Give Up.

Ruth steers her baby blue sedan toward the deserted intersection. Heading home from a taxing day in the Federal Building, she looks right. She glances left. And then…

Wham!

Before she can blink or think, a truck swerves past her and dumps three gigantic cotton bales onto the hood of her new Buick. Her slight, 5-foot-2-inch frame ricochets off the steering wheel like a pinball. Her sunglasses fling onto the dash. And her new ride is crushed. That has to hurt!

Dazed but not confused, Ruth realizes her afternoon challenges aren't over. They have just begun. And Ruth is driven by a passion more powerful than her 8-cylinder engine. As you navigate toward your next destination, reflect on the Gwinn Ten. And when the world dumps gigantic bales of cotton onto your shiny new Buick, speak oft with thy LORD!

Written in Loving Dedication to

Ruth Gwinn Martino

THE GWINN TEN

1) Thou shalt not think *too* highly of thyself.

2) Thou shalt love the LORD with all thy heart.

3) Thou shalt not fear.

4) Thou shalt honor thy father and thy mother.

5) Thou shalt not forget from whence thou came.

6) Thou shalt love thy neighbor as thyself.

7) Thou shalt work as though thou art serving the LORD.

8) Thou shalt love thy children.

9) Thou shalt not give up.

10) Thou shalt take time to be holy. Speak oft with thy LORD.

In Closing...

In Closing...

Sometimes It Takes a Bluegrass Village –

Valentine Patrick Martino

November 14, 1931 – November 12, 2019

It was the right day.

It was the appointed hour.

Yet the phone never rang.

For years, we thought we'd known what to expect.

"GOOD morning, Olivia!" was the nearly daily ritual that our daughter with autism had come to anticipate. And then on that sunny Tuesday morn, we encountered the most unpredictable of events. Absolute silence.

For those of you who have unexpectedly lost a loved one, you know what I mean.

So who was Valentine? He was my father, the product of a broken home where they spoke broken English – and not even that very well. As best I can tell, Valentine was one of 10 Italian children left to fend for themselves in the depths of the Great Depression. Valentine grew up without a mother.

You may relate to this type of challenging experience. As I was growing up, I didn't understand. I tried hard to make him feel like part of our family. He was typically detached and distant.

For most of my life, Valentine was a notorious loner. After my mother passed away, Valentine began to evolve. Perhaps out of necessity.

Somewhere near the age of 76, Valentine became one of the most gregarious guys in town. At the ripe young age of 87, he was going strong – many nights long past the midnight hour. Singing. Dancing. Flirting. He began hanging out and somehow fitting in with a posse of people who were a fraction of his age. He turned into the life of their robust party. True to form, I was dumbfounded.

So what happened? I don't know.

After eight decades of unwinding a tangled life, I believe that one of the changes that occurred for my father was his engagement with the people in a community known simply as Bluegrass Village. Somehow, it turned out to be the ideal environment to bring out his long-stifled personality. Who would have known?

Bluegrass Village has a diverse atmosphere that grounded my father. After 80 years, Valentine was finally ready to connect.

Marilyn is the lady in charge. And Marilyn has dedicated her life to building an inclusive community where everyone feels valued. She too, is on a mission!

Thank you, Marilyn, for uniting that special community! And thank you for taking my father under your wing. Your leadership and your love for each member of your community is remarkable.

In Closing...

I attended a small luncheon, which was a memorial held in honor of Valentine a few days ago. It was a simple affair. Yet, I was stunned by the enthusiasm of the crowd. Valentine's neighbors described in heartfelt enthusiasm the inspiration they drew from seeing him passionately pursuing an increasingly active lifestyle. He seemed to be picking up speed with his outlandish fashion statements. And they loved it!

One of his neighbors, Larry, shared his connection with my father in this way. He said, "Every time I see your father drive away in his car, I say to myself, 'Yep, there I go! That's me!'"

As I thought about how hard I had tried to get my father to move to Texas, I realized it was fruitless. Valentine had become more and more adamant about staying at Bluegrass Village as the years rolled by.

And for a boy who grew up on his own in the steel town of Pittsburgh, my father seemed to have finally come to appreciate the reality of a mighty three-word phrase: ***United We Stand.***

Thank you, Marilyn!

Keith Martino's leadership strategies and articles can be found in many business publications. A few of these journals include:

- *American Business Women's Association*
- *American Express Open Magazine*
- *Amsterdam Business Magazine*
- *Arizona Business Magazine / AZ Big Media*
- *Builder Magazine*
- *Central NY Business Journal*
- *Circuits Assembly Magazine*
- *Commercial Construction and Renovation Magazine*
- *Construction Business Owner Magazine*
- *Custom Home Magazine*
- *Entrepreneur Magazine*
- *FedEx Manager's Pak – Worldwide Edition*
- *For Construction Pros.com*
- *Global Man Magazine*
- *Global Woman Magazine*
- *Hot Wires Magazine*
- *Institute of Industrial and Systems Engineers Monthly*
- *LinkedIn – The Leadership Perspective*
- *London Business Magazine*
- *Modern Contractor Solutions*
- *NewsMax Magazine*
- *Remodeling Magazine*
- *Trucking News Online*
- *Women in Technology International News*
- *Young Upstarts Online Magazine*

Visit www.KeithMartino.com

Acknowledgements

As we close this book, I can't help but remember all of the friends, family and exceptional people who shared ideas and stories to make this book possible.

First, "thank you" to those who inspired me along the way. I will never underestimate the power of their positive influence.

Aretha Franklin	Brad Beldon	Chip Harper
Debbie Tripod	Dickie Deising	Dr. Peter Drucker
Dr. Thomas J. Stanley	Ed Bonneau	Eddy Ketchersid
Frederick W. Smith	Glyn (Buck) Gore	Greg Hext
Jerry Smith	Juan Pacheco	Julie Kelly
Lee Loughnane	Lou Holtz	Luke Allmon
Max Lucado	Melvin Gwinn	Michael Beldon
Rob Lowe	Robert Thompson	Ruth Martino
Valentine Martino	Waldon Gwinn	Wallace Moorehand

Please join us in a hearty salute to James (Jim) Cavanaugh, PMP for bringing his quiet gift of leadership to the table. Jim's eye for detail and relentless pursuit of excellence enabled us to make our books more succinct, accurate and engineer-friendly. Thanks JC!

And then there is the special chorus of lovely ladies who make me want to sing every time I'm with them – Olivia, Laura and Melody Martino. I love them dearly.

A super special shout out to the one person who makes my life and every book complete, my soul mate for over four delightful decades, Terri Martino.

And finally, most of all... to God be the glory.
Great things He has done!

www.ingramcontent.com/pod-product-compliance
Lightning Source LLC
Chambersburg PA
CBHW050204170426
42811CB00130B/2202/J